Moving

FORWARD

INSPIRATION FOR THE GO-GETTER JESUS GIRL

*Grace~
I pray this book blesses you as you follow your God-dreams!
Blessings~
Christa Hutch*

CHRISTA HUTCHINS

Moving Forward: Inspiration for the Go-Getter Jesus Girl

© Christa Hutchins 2019

www.DoANewThing.com

ISBN: 9781695574182

Independently published through Kindle Direct Publishing.

Cover design by Kate DiZio www.resurrectingshe.com

Editing by Liz Giertz www.LizGiertz.com

Formatting by Eswari Kamireddy on Fiverr

Dedication

To the Guest Family Girls - Mary, Dorrie, Gina, Katie, Lillie, Ruthie, Georgie and Shana - who have all taught me something about going and getting,

Special Acknowledgements

The Proverbs 31 Ministries Online Bible Studies Team - Lisa, Melissa, Kendra, Beth, Jessie, Wendy, Katrina, Kristy, and Stela - You saw something long before I did. Your love and friendship mean the world to me.

My friends who are like family - Kim, Lori, and Sally - you are the exceptions to page 81.

The Do A New Thing and Move Forward Mastermind community - I'm astounded by all you do to expand God's kingdom, and honored you allow me to be part of it.

Katie, Drew, Brandt, and Emerson - You make me proud to be Mom, Mrs. C, and G-ma.

Marty - It's not easy being married to a go-getter for more than 30 years. Thank you for loving me and reminding me that not everything is a project.

Table of Contents

Forward

I can't seem to write this without tears. I've been working for so long to become something I forgot that *I already am something.*

As a Jesus Girl chasing my calling I can't help but feel like I'm never done. In this world of writing and speaking there's always a whole list of things I could do, should do. A new deadline, website issues, email lists, marketing. I feel like I'm never going to arrive. And that has left me soul-weary as I chase my calling.

That's why I'm a bit teary. I've traded in chasing God for chasing a dream. I'm here doing the work I feel like God has called me to, but I'm so worn out. I thought pursuing my calling would feel different. Maybe not rainbows and unicorns different, but something close.

Christa understands the tension of wanting to serve God and getting caught up in the hustle of it all. And she has a better way.

Moving Forward: Inspiration for the Go-Getter Jesus Girl offers a chance to fill our tanks and teaches us how to stop running toward our calling on empty. Instead, we are reminded through Scripture, wisdom, and thoughtful questions that God is in the work, every bit of it. We are encouraged to stop hustling on our own, and instead invite God to help us do what He designed us for.

I'm ready to marry my to-do list with God's to-do list.

I'm ready to let go of my ideas in favor of God's ideas.

I'm ready to feel the exhale that comes when I remember that God is living in me so I don't have to keep striving to get to Him.

Our work is full of decisions, questions about what path to take, worrying about how we can possibly get the right things done. God wants to be in all of it. He's just waiting for us to ask.

It's time for our work to look different. It's time for our work to fill our souls. It's time for a new thing. Are you ready?

Rebecca Hastings

www.RebeccaHastings.net

Introduction

Hello, Friend.

If this little book has landed in your hands, I know something about you.

You are smart, determined, fun-loving, generous, and full of dreams, ideas, and plans.

You love Jesus and want Him to be honored and glorified by all areas of your life.

You are a go-getter Jesus girl. Me, too.

But sometimes we forget to bring Jesus into all the going and the getting. It's not really that we forget. It's more that we just don't think about involving Him in the every day decisions of business and ministry.

We are pretty good about going to the Bible for guidance on relationships or parenting, grief, disappointment, or fear ... all of those "soft" areas of our lives. But we don't always go there for guidance on strategy, planning, or which software program to choose.

Yes, I believe God wants to be part of those things. Not because He especially prefers one software program over another. But because He cares about how we make those decisions.

The things we value and prioritize and make room for matter to Him.

So this book opens the door to let Jesus into those places. It's divided into four sections: Dream A Dream, Make A Plan, Find Your People, Do The Thing. When it comes down to it, those are the four essential steps of working out any idea. You don't have to read them in order. Just jump to whichever section most applies to where you are today.

My prayer for you is that you'll see God's hand in the challenges as you move forward in ministry or business. And once you've seen it, you'll be equipped to seek out the practical wisdom He's given us in His Word.

Go change the world. Get things done with excellence. Follow Jesus in each step.

That's what it means to be a Go-Getter Jesus girl.

Dream A Dream

Dreams are fragile, yet rooted in strength.

Whispered in your heart as you lay in the dark, and shouted from rooftops in the bright sunshine.

Meant for the common good, but intensely personal.

Dreams are born out of our greatest struggles and lead to our most triumphant victories.

If you've ever dreamed a God-sized dream, you know of what I speak.

Your dream is the starting point of a fantastical journey of faith and growth. It must be protected, nurtured, developed and above all, it must be treasured as a gift from God to you and those it will eventually impact.

So dream a dream, girl. A glorious adventure is in front of you. So let's get you moving forward.

WHEN GOD
ASKS US TO
WAIT, HE
ASKS US TO
TRUST HIM

WAITING OR PROCRASTINATING?

Yes, Lord, walking in the way of your laws, we wait for you; your name and renown are the desires of our heart. Isaiah 26:8 (NIV)

"I'm waiting for God's timing on that." Have you said that before? I know I have. Usually with a martyr's sigh and the back of my hand to my forehead, ready to swoon with exhaustion from …. doing nothing.

Many times we truly *are* waiting on God before moving forward. We wait for Him to prepare us for a big assignment. We wait for Him to unlock a door. We wait for God to make it clear it's time for a change. We wait. And we wait. And it is good.

But sometimes, we use "waiting" as an excuse … as a euphemism for procrastinating. The challenge God has put in front of us is so big, so audacious, we just can't wrap our heads around it. It's so complicated and needs such focus it will take super-human effort to do it right. So we wait. And we wait. And it is procrastinating.

How do we know the difference? How do we know if we are obediently waiting for God's timing, or if we are avoiding the new thing He has called us to do?

God-ordained waiting brings a hopeful excitement. Something big on the horizon is going to change everything and because God is in it, we know it is worth the wait. Procrastination brings a burdensome dread. Something is not getting done; an opportunity is being missed. If we don't get up and do what God has called us to do, the loss will be crushing.

When God asks us to wait, He asks us to trust Him. He knows when the time is right and we turn to Him before we move right or move left so He will be honored by our steps. The fear of failure will cause us to put things off, being more concerned about how we will look than how God will move.

Waiting can be a productive time of refreshing, preparing, and drawing closer to God. But when God says, "Go," it's time to jump in with our whole hearts, all of our energy, and a trust that knows even if we fail, God's got our backs.

Forward Thinking

Are you in a time of waiting or procrastinating?

What clues will you use to tell which is which?

OUTSIDE OUR
COMFORT
ZONE, WE
LEARN TO
TRUST AND
GAIN THE
ASSURANCE
THAT ONLY
GOD CAN
MAKE IT
HAPPEN

OUT OF OUR COMFORT ZONES

You go before me and follow me. You place your hand of blessing on my head. Psalm 139:5 (NLT)

Most of us are creatures of habit. We like to stay where the routine is reliable, the people are familiar, and the place is comfortable. But have you noticed how God is always sending people out of their comfort zones?

Think about Moses. In Exodus 6:28-7:7 God asked him to speak on behalf of His enslaved people. But Moses was uncomfortable and afraid that his words would be jumbled. God's suggestion that Aaron could be the spokesperson helped Moses move out of his comfort zone and equipped Moses to take on the role of leader.

What about Ananias in Acts 9:10–19? God asked him to take a message to Saul, who you might remember had a nasty reputation as a Christ-hater and persecutor of Christians. But God knew more than Ananias. He knew there was a special plan for Saul-who-would-become-Paul—a plan that Saul was now ready to receive. Ananias was obedient, stepped out of his comfort zone to do what God told him to do, and the rest is history …. literally.

Sometimes God goes before us, providing resources that help us step out. Other times, He follows behind us, gently whispering encouragement in our ears because He sees what we cannot see. Either way, He usually does not want us to stay where we are, in the place where we are comfortable.

Inside the comfort zone, we can depend on our own abilities and efforts. God doesn't need to show up with supernatural provision, because we have everything closely controlled. We don't need to be dependent on Him when our confidence is in familiar people and places.

Outside our comfort zone, we learn to trust and gain the assurance that only God can make it happen. It is there that we let go of everything familiar to grasp His hand of blessing.

Forward Thinking

Where is God nudging you out of your comfort zone?

How is He equipping you or giving you confidence to follow Him into the unknown?

How might you grow if you follow where He is leading?

WHEN WE HAVE
NOT CONNECTED
WITH GOD'S
SPECIFIC PLAN
FOR OUR
DREAMS, WE
CAST OFF THE
RESTRAINTS OF
DISCIPLINE,
PLANNING, AND
CONSISTENCY

DEFINE SUCCESS

Where there is no vision, the people perish. Proverbs 29:18 (KJV)

Many a motivational guru has quoted this verse, hoping to inspire leaders to cast a vision of success for their teams or followers. Recently, I heard Dave Ramsey say this is not a verse about vision; it is a warning about perishing. It's much more personal than a team-building exercise.

We usually quote the King James Version of this verse, but the New International Version has a very different feel.

"Where there is no revelation, people cast off restraint." (NIV)

In fact, instead of "vision," most modern translations say "revelation," "guidance," or "prophetic vision." The word refers to a special revelation from God.

And how about the word for "perishing"? It doesn't necessarily mean death or destruction. It is more like the chaos that comes when there are no ground rules or guidance. In fact, the rest of the verse says, "but blessed is he who follows the law." (ESV)

So this verse really is a warning about what happens when we move forward in our own strength, without a revelation or guidance from God. When we have not connected with God's specific plan for our dreams, we cast off the restraints of discipline, planning, and consistency. Overwhelm moves in as we try to follow the conflicting advice of all the "experts." We wander around aimlessly, confused about what to do next, wasting time and resources.

Things quickly spiral into chaos. Our motivation dies. Our dream perishes.

But if we tune in to how God defines success for us, it may look different than we expect. He will clarify the next steps and lead us to the specific resources we need. When we faithfully, consistently do the things He has instructed us to do, we will know the blessing of His guidance.

Don't allow your dreaming and goal setting to default to a purely mental exercise based on worldly rules and standards that define success. Spend time in prayer and contemplation, asking God for a revelation so your next steps will be orderly instead of chaotic.

Forward Thinking

What revelation has God given you for your dream?

Has He given you a vision for all He wants you to achieve?

GOD MAY HAVE
BIGGER PLANS
FOR YOUR
CALLING THAN
YOU THINK

EMBRACE YOUR CALLING TO LEADERSHIP

And we also thank God continually because, when you received the word of God, which you heard from us, you accepted it not as a human word, but as it actually is, the word of God, which is indeed at work in you who believe. 1 Thessalonians 2:13 (NIV)

How do people get to be "leaders"? We often think of the person who calls the shots as the "leader." But "leadership" is not a position. Many people have the organizational skills, attention to detail, and people power to pull off a project on time and on budget, but that doesn't necessarily make them leaders.

Leadership is a way of moving through the world that makes others want to follow. Leaders can be found in every part of an organization, from the corner office to the cubicle. In fact, if there are NOT leaders where the work is actually getting done, the whole thing may fall apart.

Now, you might be smugly thinking this leadership thing doesn't apply to you. After all, God called you to write a book or start a blog or sell the products you and your kids are making in your basement, not start a church, for goodness sakes! But you would be wrong. (#sorrynotsorry)

You see, God may have bigger plans for your calling than you think. He may use your everyday interactions—your small victories and painful failures—to lead others in ways you can't imagine.

You wouldn't have seen much leadership potential in the first century church. They were just regular people with the same struggles, limitations, bad attitudes, and failures as everyone else. But those flawed people did extraordinary things because they learned the lifestyle of leadership by watching Jesus, Paul, Peter, and the others.

That's the same for every leader there has ever been. Leaders are just regular, flawed people who have learned to look above the present situation and find the way through it. That awareness is unique to good leaders. Knowing their leader is looking out ahead to make the way clear gives people the confidence to follow them.

Whether you are leading an organization with multiple layers or leading yourself to set the course of your mini-ministry, you can grow into the leader God needs you to be.

Forward Thinking

Who are you leading right now?

What qualities of leadership do you most need to develop?

Where is God calling you to lead next?

WHEN WE SEEK
TO BE OBEDIENT
TO GOD'S
PURPOSE FOR
OUR LIVES, WE
CAN REST
CONFIDENTLY IN
HIS VISION

WHEN DOUBT ATTACKS YOUR PURPOSE

But I prayed, "Now strengthen my hands." Nehemiah 6:9 (NIV)

If you've ever pursued purpose, you have certainly encountered doubt. Sometimes, doubt comes as hurtful rumors from people who don't believe in what you are doing. Other times, it comes as frightening thoughts that shake your confidence.

However it comes, we don't have to give in to the soul-crushing fear that often follows doubt.

When we are confident in God's calling and are walking in faithful obedience to our purpose, we can stand up to those internal or external attacks, just like Nehemiah did.

God instructed Nehemiah to rebuild the wall laying in ruins around Jerusalem. Nehemiah rallied the citizens of Jerusalem to dedicate themselves to the task.

But Nehemiah's plans were not without opposition. When doubt and fear tried to attack him with rumors and frightening thoughts, Nehemiah stood in his purpose with confidence.

The local leaders accused Nehemiah of plotting a revolt and appointing prophets to announce him as king (Nehemiah 6:6-7). They did not understand his mission, and made up their own version of Nehemiah's story.

Nehemiah clapped back with one of the snappiest lines in the Bible.

"Nothing like what you are saying is happening; you are just making it up out of your head." Nehemiah 6:8 (NIV)

Nehemiah spoke truth into the situation. He did not allow others to fill in the gaps and tell their version of his story. He also recognized the tactics of his enemies.

They were all trying to frighten us, thinking, "Their hands will get too weak for the work, and it will not be completed. But I prayed, "Now strengthen my hands." Nehemiah 6:9 (NIV)

Nehemiah prayed for God to strengthen his hands—to build him up in the exact place doubt was attacking.

Often, when the enemy plants frightening thoughts in our hearts, our first response is to doubt our calling. "God, did You REALLY call me to this? Did I REALLY hear from You on this assignment?" But Nehemiah demonstrates a better way.

You can't do this because you aren't smart enough.
God, strengthen my mind and be my Teacher.

You can't afford to do this.
God, strengthen my finances and be my Provider.

You can't do this because you don't have any help.
God, strengthen my connections and be my Helper.

When we seek to be obedient to God's purpose for our lives, we can rest confidently in His vision and faithfully ask for His strength, instead of constantly begging for confirmation.

By speaking truth and praying for strength, Nehemiah stood up to doubt and inspired a nation to do what his enemies said was impossible.

Forward Thinking

When doubt attacks, are you able to stand up to it?

How does Nehemiah's example inspire you today?

THE ONLY LINE
WE CAN
MEASURE
OURSELVES
AGAINST IS THE
LINE GOD HAS
DRAWN IN
SCRIPTURE

WHEN YOUR DREAMING FEELS LIKE SCHEMING

We always thank God for all of you, mentioning you in our prayers. We continually remember before our God and Father your work produced by faith, your labor prompted by love and your endurance inspired by hope in our Lord Jesus Christ. For we know, brothers and sisters loved by God, that he has chosen you. 1 Thessalonians 1:2-4 (NIV)

As ministry leaders and Go-Getter Jesus girls with big dreams, we often struggle to find the line between dreaming and scheming. How do we know when we are pursuing our dreams in a way that honors God and His calling on our lives versus when we are scheming for self-promotion?

There is a lot of talk in the Christian blogosphere about platforms and promotion and personal branding. What is considered good practice for some is called "justification" by others. The well-defined line we all are looking for does not exist.

So the only line we can measure ourselves against is the line God has drawn in Scripture. That line runs straight from His Word through our hearts and our motives.

As we read above, Paul starts his letter to the leaders of the Thessalonican church by commending them for their faithful work, labors of love, and hopeful endurance. His words show us how to grow our ministries in ways that honor God and His calling.

Work produced by faith means trusting God for the results. It's doing what is right and reasonable without getting consumed by numbers or responding to even small bits of success with pride.

Labor prompted by love serves other people. It meets the needs of the hurting, confused, and broken. When our actions are prompted by love, our main concern is walking through a transformation with the people we serve.

Endurance inspired by hope in Jesus keeps us dependent on His constant direction, provision, and peace. There are no real "overnight sensations" (well, Chewbacca Mom might be the exception); for most of us, it takes consistent faithfulness over a long period of time. It takes endurance.

He chose you. He gave you a passion to share your heart out of love and a desire to serve. Embrace that calling and keep your eyes on the hope of Jesus Christ. Your dream will become the vehicle God uses to advance His kingdom, not simply a scheme to advance your own.

Forward Thinking

What moves you to action?

What drives you to try new things in ministry?

Examine your motivations; are they honoring God's calling on your life?

GOD WILL
PROVIDE ALL
YOU NEED TO
DO ALL THAT
HE'S CALLED
YOU TO DO

STAY COMMITTED TO YOUR SACRED GOALS

The Lord will fulfill his purpose for me; your steadfast love, O Lord, endures forever. Do not forsake the work of your hands. Psalm 138:8 (ESV)

Sitting by a crackling fire on New Year's Eve with a cup of hot cocoa and a blank planner, it's easy to set goals for the next year. They are significant, sacred even, because they aren't just our goals; they are God's goals for us.

You'd think having eternal significance on our minds would be enough to keep us committed to them. But by the time we are dying Easter eggs and attending passion plays, we've often lost our focus on those sacred goals.

To re-spark your passion for a goal gone cold, remember why you set it. There was a transformation needed, progress to make, change to find, and you have the unique abilities and experience God will use to make it happen. Remind yourself what moving forward to meet this goal will allow you to do—not just in your own life, but also in the lives of others.

It might be even more important to remind yourself what happens if you don't meet this goal. I'm not talking about self-imposed penalties like a dollar in the cuss jar if you can't control your mouth. I mean what happens in your soul if you step away from what God so strongly laid on your heart. The damage caused by not making progress in one area can put up roadblocks to growth in any other area of your life.

Commitment comes at a cost. Reaching your goal will require time, accountability, resources, and inspiration. I've said it many times before—if you don't have enough time to do all the things God has called you to do, you are doing things He didn't intend for you to do. The same is true with all the other resources you need. God will provide all you need to do all that He's called you to do. It's just that simple.

Pursuing your goal will require some soul-searching and sacrifice. Maintaining your passion for your dream, much like keeping those flames crackling in the fireplace late into the night, may be lonely and difficult. But it is worth it.

What has caused your passion for your goals to wane?

What can you do spark the sacred fires of commitment again?

Resources for Dreamers

Visit www.doanewthing.com/gogetter for additional resources related to this book.

Download the **Define Success Worksheet** to help you set Good, Better, Best goals

Get the **Goal Declaration Worksheet** to keep your sacred goals in front of you.

Make A Plan

How do you feel about making plans? If you tend towards "Type A," you call your planner your "brain" and feel lost without a detailed to-do list for each day. My "Type B" friends feel fenced in by a strict agenda and spend more time decorating their planner with washi tape and stickers than they do actually making plans.

Somewhere in between is a healthier place. A good plan gives you confidence that things are not falling through the cracks and offers flexibility when conditions change.

Join me as we look to God's Word to find that healthier place.

WE HAVE A
RESPONSIBILITY
TO PLAN WELL
AND MAKE THE
BEST USE OF
OUR RESOURCES

THE POWER OF SUCCESSFUL PROJECTS

And Joseph went out from Pharaoh's presence and traveled throughout Egypt. During the seven years of abundance the land produced plentifully. Joseph collected all the food produced in those seven years of abundance in Egypt and stored it in the cities. In each city he put the food grown in the fields surrounding it. Joseph stored up huge quantities of grain, like the sand of the sea; it was so much that he stopped keeping records because it was beyond measure.
Genesis 41:46-49

Joseph's life was not an easy one. He was sold into slavery by his brothers, separated from his family for years, falsely accused of sexual assault, and thrown into prison. But God had a special project for Joseph - one that would change not only his life, but the lives of the Egyptians and the future nation of Israel.

God gave Joseph the wisdom to interpret Pharaoh's dream and knew there would be seven years of abundance followed by seven years of extreme famine. Joseph was put in charge of preparing for the famine. He showed all the signs of managing the project well.

He did his research. Before putting any plans in place, Joseph surveyed the land to understand the size of the problem and the resources available to him.

He had a schedule. Most projects are time-bound and Joseph's was no exception. He had seven years of plenty to prepare for seven years of famine.

He had a plan to use his resources. Imagine the logistical arrangements required to store grain for seven years! Joseph mobilized the local people to secure storage space year after year. By having each city store the food grown in their surrounding fields, he empowered the people to control their own successful future.

Joseph's project was successful. When the famine started, the Egyptians had so much food that people from the surrounding countries traveled to Egypt to purchase grain.

As leaders, we have a responsibility to plan well and make the best use of our resources. Our team counts on us. Our dream counts on us.

What if Joseph's project had not been well-planned or set up for success? Would the Egyptians have starved, changing the political and social landscape? We'll never know. But we do know that because of Joseph's successful project, he was reunited with his family and the scarlet thread that leads to Christ was woven through another generation.

Forward Thinking

What ideas or tasks on your plate would be more successful if they were planned as a project?

What impact would those successful projects have on your ministry?

LET'S WALK
WITH HIM AND
WORK WITH HIM
AND LEARN HOW
HE DOES IT

UNFORCED RHYTHMS

Are you tired? Worn out? Burned out on religion? Come to me. Get away with me and you'll recover your life. I'll show you how to take a real rest. Walk with me and work with me—watch how I do it. Learn the unforced rhythms of grace. I won't lay anything heavy or ill-fitting on you. Keep company with me and you'll learn to live freely and lightly. Matthew 11:28-30 (MSG)

When I first read The Message version of this well-known verse, I felt my soul unfurl a little. It was an almost physical release of years of expectations, requirements, and self-imposed rules designed for me to keep up with the race.

The idea that I could "learn to live freely and lightly" felt completely foreign to me. Living was anything but free and light. It was full of deadlines, juggling home and work, and feeling guilty that I was doing none of it well.

The part that stood out was this:

"Learn the unforced rhythms of grace."

When it comes to my time, everything seems forced.

I'm forced to spend a couple of hours every day cooking and cleaning.

I'm forced to spend forty hours or more every week at work.

I'm forced to spend three hours every month getting my graying hair colored (the struggle is real, y'all!).

But when I thought about it, I still had a lot of hours left over that were "unforced." What was I doing with the unforced hours? Was I using them intentionally? Was I tending to each area of my life in its own rhythm?

Jesus didn't say to "balance" our time or to give to each area equally. No, He encouraged us to pay attention to the unforced rhythms. Some things naturally rise to the top of our priorities for a season and then sink lower at other times.

It doesn't come easily or naturally. We watch how Jesus did it and learn from Him. Sometimes He pushed in to the crowd and met their needs, even against the advice of His closest friends and followers. Other times, He retreated for alone time, even with the need was great.

He practiced rhythms, not balance. Let's walk with Him and work with Him and learn how He does it.

Forward Thinking

What things are at the top of your priority rhythm right now?

What heavy or ill-fitting things are you trying to carry?

What can you learn about how Jesus handled others' expectations?

WHEN OUR
CONFIDENCE IS
IN GOD, OUR
PLANS CAN BE
MOLDED TO FILL
IN THE SPACE
HE IS PUSHING
US TOWARDS

IS YOUR CONFIDENCE IN YOUR PLANS?

For I know the plans I have for you," declares the Lord, "plans to prosper you and not to harm you, plans to give you hope and a future. Jeremiah 29:11 (NIV)

The Bible seems to be conflicted about planning. On the one hand, it says it is wise to plan ahead.

> *A wise man thinks ahead; a fool doesn't, and even brags about it! Proverbs 13:16 (TLB)*

On the other hand, it says don't worry; put your plans in God's hands.

> *So don't be anxious about tomorrow. God will take care of your tomorrow, too. Live one day at a time. Matthew 6:34 (TLB)*

But as the well-loved verse from Jeremiah says, God has made plans for us. That is good news for this mama who printed individual schedule cards for each person in our party the last time we went to Disney World! So if God is a planner, it can't be all wrong, can it?

James helps us sort it out:

> *Look here, you people who say, "Today or tomorrow we are going to such and such a town, stay there a year, and open up a profitable business." How do you know what is going to happen tomorrow? For the length of your lives is*

as uncertain as the morning fog—now you see it; soon it is gone. What you ought to say is, "If the Lord wants us to, we shall live and do this or that." Otherwise you will be bragging about your own plans, and such self-confidence never pleases God. James 4:13-16 (TLB).

Planning is not a problem. Putting our confidence in our plans rather than in God is a problem. When we put our confidence in our plans, we get grumpy when things don't go according to them, we push past people to protect our projects, and we count ourselves as failures when our plans fall through.

When our confidence is in God, our plans can be molded to fill in the space He is pushing us towards. In excited anticipation, we ask Him "What next?" when our carefully laid plans get jumbled.

Forward Thinking

Where is your confidence? In God? Or in your plans?

What plans may need to be put aside in response to your confidence in God?

WHETHER IT IS
OUR TIME,
MONEY, OR
KNOWLEDGE,
OUR DREAMS
WILL COST US
SOMETHING
VALUABLE

IDENTIFY YOUR RESOURCE NEEDS

As each has received a gift, use it to serve one another, as good stewards of God's varied grace. 1 Peter 4:10 (ESV)

Sometimes I wonder what I could I do with my dreams if I had unlimited resources.

If I had all the time I needed, instead of precious minutes snatched from lunch hours, before-the-sun-is-up mornings, and late nights when the house is quiet?

If I had all the money I needed to hire help, instead of letting the must-be-dones rob me of time and energy for my passions.

If I knew how to do everything, instead of figuring it out as I go and making awkward work-arounds because I don't know a better way.

You may have also felt the sting of limited resources, of feeling left behind others who make it look so easy. In reality, none of us has unlimited resources, and I suspect if we did, we would be totally overwhelmed by all the possibilities.

I've allowed my perceived lack of resources to stop me in my tracks at times. But I've come to view that needy space as God's protection and my opportunity to experience His provision.

No matter what we feel we lack, God will provide all the resources we need to do the thing He called us to do. It's possible they won't be what we expected, and we may need to consider creative ways to use what we already have.

Our resources of time, money, and experience work like a triangle where abundance in some areas can balance out a gap in another. Financial resources can pay for an assistant and allow us to extend our time. Or our skills can generate income to pay the expenses of a growing online presence. Recognize the value of what you have at hand and find creative ways to use it.

Resources are precious. Whether it is our time, money, or knowledge, our dreams will cost us something valuable.

So let's make it worth that cost. Giving God control of all our resources and being dependent on Him to provide ensures our resources will be used wisely and all our gaps will be filled. Instead of fretting over what you don't have, focus on what you do.

Forward Thinking

What everyday resources are available to be used for greater impact?

How can you use what you have to fill the gaps of what you lack?

WHAT COULD I DO WITH TEN MINUTES IF I WAS BEING INTENTIONAL?

HOW DO YOU MAKE JUST TEN MINUTES MATTER?

We must quickly carry out the tasks assigned us by the one who sent us. The night is coming, and then no one can work. John 9:4 (NLT)

Our days are busy; we constantly rush from one task to another errand. There is not enough time in the day for all the things we need to do, whether for work, for ministry, or for family.

But every once in a while (and if we are honest, more often than we care to admit), a random burst of time pops up unexpectedly in our day.

10 minutes until time to leave the house for an appointment, 10 minutes to wait in a carpool line, 10 minutes before the next meeting.

What do we do with those short minutes? I don't know about you, but I have become more and more aware of how often I waste them. I grab my phone and check Facebook, play a level of Candy Crush (am I the only one on the planet still playing Candy Crush?), or walk to the vending machine for a diet Coke. I let those precious 10-minute moments slip through my fingers because I think 10 minutes isn't long enough to accomplish any "real" work.

What if I could snatch back the short bits of time so easily wasted and use them in purposeful ways for myself, my ministry, and my family? What could I do with 10 minutes if I was being intentional? I want to steward well every opportunity God gives me.

I find it helpful to keep a list of quick and easy things to do in the Notes app on my phone, so when I get one of those pops of time, I don't waste half of it figuring out what I could do.

Then, at the end of the day when no more work can be done, I can rest with satisfaction that I have accomplished all I could for the Lord in that day. And wake up the next day with intention to do it again. Because every moment matters.

What could you do with your 10 minutes? Make a list and keep it handy.

What time-wasters do you need to intentionally avoid?

WE LOOK AT
MISTAKES AS
FAILURES WHEN
THEY ARE
REALLY
OPPORTUNITIES
IN DISGUISE

FIXING THE SOFT SPOTS

We all make many mistakes. James 3:2a (NLT)

It's hard to look at the things that aren't going so well … the places where we fell short of our expectations, where we did not (or could not) follow through on the things we committed to do.

It could be a time when the enemy starts to take jabs in your head.

"See, I told you you couldn't do this."

"You have no idea what you are doing."

"God will never be able to use a mess like you."

We can only fix the things we know about, so taking a close look at each stumble is an important part of growing. Before you even have a chance to entertain those lies, I want to remind you of two simple, yet profound, truths.

Mistakes are healthy growth opportunities. Of course, we know that everyone makes mistakes. There was only one perfect Person. But why do our own mistakes always seem more painful, more costly, and more embarrassing than anyone else's? Because we look at mistakes as failures when they are really opportunities in disguise.

If we step away from our mistakes and observe them from all angles, we find truth we could not learn otherwise. We see ways we can improve, or things we could have done differently, things that set us on a more successful path.

God doesn't leave us when we stumble. The Bible says several times that God upholds the righteous when they fall.

The Lord makes firm the steps of the one who delights in him; though he may stumble, he will not fall, for the Lord upholds him with his hand. Psalm 37:23-24 (NIV)

He will be right there with us, helping us fix whatever is not working, making our soft spots firm. He'll remind us we are defined not by our mistakes, or even by our reaction to them, but by His love for us.

So kick the enemy out of your head before you start looking at your mistakes. Invite the Holy Spirit to bring truth to your mind as you consider how to grow from them.

Forward Thinking

What soft areas of your ministry need some focus?

How do you see God encouraging you in those areas?

WHEN THE
DESTINATION
SEEMS FAR
AWAY,
MILESTONES
REMIND US
THAT WE ARE
MAKING
PROGRESS

MARKING YOUR MILESTONES

Set up road markers for yourself; make yourself guideposts; consider well the highway, the road by which you went.
Jeremiah 31:21 (ESV)

On a long car journey, we start off focused on the destination. We want to get there-- to that sunny vacation spot, or that house full of relatives waiting for us with open arms and a warm hug.

But shortly after we leave, we start looking for the mile markers, the modern day milestones. They tell us how far we have gone and how far we have left to go. They also serve as a reference point to let us know we are on the right path.

When the destination seems far away, milestones remind us that we are making progress. In 1 Samuel 7:12, Samuel named his milestone "Ebenezer," meaning "Thus far has the Lord helped us." As you are following God into your calling, marking your milestones allows you to optimize the map to your destination.

Milestones don't have to be based on tasks completed.

- A first blog post written
- A follower count exceeded
- A number on the scale met

Milestones can also be significant spiritual points on our journey.

- A heart turned towards God
- A stronghold overcome
- Persevering to the end of a hard season
- Being one bit more like Jesus

It may seem like these spiritual milestones are overlooked. But scripture reminds that they are very seen:

For God is not unjust so as to overlook your work and the love that you have shown for his name in serving the saints, as you still do. Hebrews 6:10 (ESV)

It encourages me to know that God is aware of our service to His saints and the way we love His people. He sees these milestones that often feel unseen.

Your plans should include strategies to reach both practical and spiritual milestones. Thus far has the Lord helped you. Now keep going towards the destination!

Forward Thinking

What significant milestones have you passed recently?

What major milestone is on your horizon?

What do you consider the strengths of your ministry?

How can you use those strengths to reach your milestone?

Resources for Planners

Visit www.doanewthing.com/gogetter for additional resources related to this book.

Download a free **How To Plan A Project** workshop video.

Get a free module on the **Resource Triangle**, including a Bible Study and training video.

Learn the **5 Reasons Your Planner Isn't Working For You.**

Check out the **Boss Your Time Around course** ... my exclusive time planning system.

Take the **Build A Better Week Challenge.**

Find Your People

Whether you are an introvert, an extrovert or an "extroverted introvert," finding the people to do ministry and life with is an important part of being a healthy leader.

God did not make us to do this alone. He made us for community. We know this, and yet, we often continue struggling by ourselves. Especially for go-getter girls like us, our mile-wide independent streak tends to make us treat other people like baggage we have to drag along, rather than valuable partners God has injected into our stories.

Come along as we explore this idea of community in both the Old and New Testaments. Kings, disciples, and wilderness wanderers all needed their community to reach their God-given purpose. And so do you!

THERE ARE
PEOPLE OUT
THERE WHO
WANT TO BE IN
COMMUNITY
WITH YOU

COMMUNITY MEANS BETTER TOGETHER

The Lord said to Moses: "Bring me seventy of Israel's elders who are known to you as leaders and officials among the people... They will share the burden of the people with you so that you will not have to carry it alone." Numbers 11:16-17 (NIV)

Leading a ministry or organization alone is manageable at first. You make a plan and get inspired, excited even! You can do this thing! Really! You can!

So you dive in with your whole heart. Things are happening. You are checking tasks off your to-do list .. totally rocking this leadership thing. Go, you!

Then you hit the wall. The registration website goes down right after your big announcement. The childcare worker gets sick and cancels at the last minute. The blog post you were carefully crafting but only half-finished mysteriously posts itself in the middle of the night. (Not that any of those things have ever happened to me ....)

Uggghhhh!!! Frustrating!! You may have lashed out at God the same way Moses did when the Israelites were driving him crazy:

I cannot carry all these people by myself; the burden is too heavy for me. If this is how you are going to treat me, please go ahead and kill me—if I have found favor in your eyes—and do not let me face my own ruin. Numbers 11:14-15 (NIV)

God gave Moses some great advice: "Get a community." Yep, God told Moses to surround himself with 70 leaders. Not only that, but God promised to uniquely equip those leaders to help Moses.

That's what a good community does for you. They don't just stand back and cheer you on. They help you and share the burden. When you are tired and whining, they don't let you give up, but they remind you of what God has called you to and why.

Look. I know it's hard sharing your biggest dreams, struggles, and insecurities with others. You feel needy and like the new girl at the party. But there are people out there who WANT to be in community with you. Who NEED to be in community to you.

If Moses needed 70 people in his community, you need at least a few, right?

Forward Thinking

What progress could you make in a community of like-minded women who support and encourage you and give you tough-grace accountability to keep (or get) going?

What barriers do you face in developing a supportive community?

What action can you take to remove the barriers?

OUR FEAR-BASED
RELUCTANCE TO
TELL PEOPLE
WHAT GOD IS
DOING COULD BE
THE BARRIER
HOLDING US
BACK

TELL SOMEBODY

Fix these words of mine in your hearts and minds...talking about them when you sit at home and when you walk along the road, when you lie down and when you get up. Deuteronomy 11:18a, 19b (NIV)

Think about the most amazing, exciting thing that has ever happened to you. Got it in your head? Now, think about your conversations around the time it happened.

I bet you worked that exciting thing into every conversation you had! It may have been just a casual mention when talking to a colleague at work. Perhaps you shared a little more of the story out by the swings on a playdate. Or maybe you spilled every heart-thumping detail over a cup of coffee with your best friend.

But who could blame you? I mean, it WAS amazing. Everyone needed to know, and you were pumped to tell them.

Then why oh why are we so reluctant to tell people when we start stepping into the dream God has given us? Is it because we are afraid we may fail? Or worry they won't care? Or we don't want to sound vain or conceited?

Our fear-based reluctance to tell people what God is doing could be the barrier holding us back. Walking where God has called us to walk is an amazing, exciting thing. We should be pumped to talk about it at home, along the road, when we lie down, and when we get up. We all have a story to share.

69

Because if we are brave enough to tell somebody, we may succeed in encouraging them to move forward in their own calling.

Because if we tell them what we need, they may care enough to walk along with us and be part of our story.

Because if we sound confident in what God is doing, they may want to experience that kind of confidence, too.

So go ahead, TELL somebody about the amazing, exciting work God is doing through you! It could be a game-changer.

What exciting things are happening in your walk and work?

Who will you share them with today?

COMMUNITY CAN BE MESSY

LIVING IN COMMUNITY

All the men and women, the people of Israel, whose heart moved them to bring anything for the work that the Lord had commanded by Moses to be done brought it as a freewill offering to the Lord. Exodus 35:29 (ESV)

When we look at examples of community in the Bible, we are naturally drawn to the account of the early church in Acts. They worshipped, ate, and lived together in harmony, devoted to the apostles and to each other.

That idyllic picture may be the goal, but in our day and age, community often looks a little rougher around the edges. Community can be messy.

The Israelites who left Egypt with Pharaoh on their heels had all the makings of a thriving community. They had a strong leader in Moses, were united in the common purpose of getting to the Promised Land, and had strength in numbers. But even with all of those advantages, living in community was messy for the Israelites. We can learn from their messiness.

Communities need guidelines. The Ten Commandments were the original group rules. Following these ten rules, which Jesus boiled down to loving God and loving people, would make the Israelites healthy and holy, an example of community that would bring God glory.

Working through hard stuff can strengthen the bond. The Israelites faced a lot of tough circumstances, including hunger, weariness, and even the death of their leader just before they reached their goal. Hard times can break a community. Some people will leave because they lose the will or the energy. But those who stay and face the hard times with honesty, valuing the community above themselves, find it easier to face the next challenge together.

Community takes divine inspiration. In Exodus 35, we read how Moses gathered materials for the tabernacle and I find the wording in this chapter very interesting: "everyone whose heart stirred him," "All who were of a willing heart," "All the men and women, the people of Israel, whose heart moved them."

As their leader for decades, Moses clearly had the authority to demand their contributions, but there was no need. After facing hardship and living in community together, the whiny, complaining bunch that crossed the Red Sea became a strong community working together towards a common goal. Only God could work that change in their hearts.

Forward Thinking

Examine your attitudes towards living in community. What aspects of community are important to you?

How can you contribute to a thriving community where you are?

MINISTRY IS
NOT A
COMPETITION

WORKING WITH FRIENDLY PARTNERS

When Hiram king of Tyre heard that Solomon had been anointed king to succeed his father David, he sent his envoys to Solomon, because he had always been on friendly terms with David. Solomon sent back this message to Hiram:

"You know that because of the wars waged against my father David from all sides, he could not build a temple for the Name of the Lord his God until the Lord put his enemies under his feet. But now the Lord my God has given me rest on every side, and there is no adversary or disaster. I intend, therefore, to build a temple for the Name of the Lord my God, as the Lord told my father David, when he said, 'Your son whom I will put on the throne in your place will build the temple for my Name.'

"So give orders that cedars of Lebanon be cut for me. My men will work with yours, and I will pay you for your men whatever wages you set. You know that we have no one so skilled in felling timber as the Sidonians." 1 Kings 5:1-6 (NIV)

After David died and Solomon became king, Solomon picked up the torch his father had left him to build the temple. But he needed help, so he responded to a letter from a friend of David's. In the verses above, notice how Solomon wisely made a deal with a friendly partner.

He recognized a gap. "We have no one so skilled in felling timber." Solomon was aware of his people's strengths and weaknesses. Rather than doing an important task poorly, he partnered with an expert.

He offered something in return. "I will pay you for your men." Working with a partner is not a one-way deal. Solomon made sure his partner would benefit from the arrangement as well.

He used it as a growth opportunity. "My men will work with yours." By working alongside the experts, Solomon's men would learn a skill and put a new tool in the Israelite's toolbox, making them more independent in the future.

Solomon used his abundant resources–manpower and food– to obtain supplies he didn't have–skillfully cut timber. And it was all possible because of strong relationships with his peers.

Ministry is not a competition. When we know each other's strengths and weaknesses and generously share our resources, we will all grow and build His kingdom. And that is way more satisfying than building our own kingdoms.

Forward Thinking

What do you have in abundance that you could use to help someone else?

What are you lacking that someone else could supply?

How would that partnership also benefit your ministry?

WE ARE
STRONGER,
BOLDER, MORE
COURAGEOUS,
MORE FAITHFUL,
AND JUST PLAIN
BETTER
TOGETHER

BUILD RELATIONSHIPS BY STAYING IN TOUCH

I long to see you so that I may impart to you some spiritual gift to make you strong— that is, that you and I may be mutually encouraged by each other's faith. Romans 1:11-12

I've moved around quite a bit during my life and, with few exceptions, I have to admit I am terrible at keeping in touch with people after I move. It's not that I don't still care about them or want to be part of their lives. It's just that I get caught up in what's in front of me. I could take some lessons from Paul.

Paul was passionate about connecting with people, and connecting people with each other. Even as he sat in a jail cell, he encouraged the early church to visit, learn from, and support one another.

Connecting with people is a two-way street. Recognizing that the Christian life is hard, Paul knew we are stronger, bolder, more courageous, more faithful, and just plain better together than we are in isolation. So his missionary journey plans always included connecting with friends, connecting his friends with each other, and building relationships with influencers who opened ministry doors for him.

But these were not self-serving relationships. In the middle of 2 Corinthians 12:14, Paul says:

I will not be a burden to you, because what I want is not your possessions but you. (NIV)

Is that not a beautiful word to speak over someone? I don't want what you can do for me. I want you. Time with you. Heart talk with you. Deep, genuine connection with you.

These deep, genuine connections gave Paul the opening he needed to greet, teach, encourage, and correct the early followers of Christ. He respected the access he was given and used it to serve others and point them to Jesus rather than promote himself. He was not building a following. He was building authentic relationships.

Authentic relationships feed souls, free spirits, and fuel efforts. Without them, ministry is lonely and lifeless.

Forward Thinking

Examine your attitudes about connecting with people. Are your connections real and authentic, or based only on what you can do for each other?

Who do you need to reach out to and re-establish connection?

IN TRUE
COMMUNITY,
THERE IS NO
SHAME IN
RECEIVING

LEVERAGE YOUR COMMUNITY

All the believers were together and had everything in common. They sold property and possessions to give to anyone who had need. Every day they continued to meet together in the temple courts. They broke bread in their homes and ate together with glad and sincere hearts, Acts 2:44-46 (NIV)

Wouldn't you have loved being a member of the early church? Those people had it going on when it came to taking care of each other and living in community. They made sure everyone had what they needed.

And based on these verses in Acts, I don't think this was one of those "bring it all to the storehouse" kind of things, where Peter and John's garage turned into a giant clothes closet for everyone to go shopping.

No, it says they "distributed the proceeds to all." I think, in this community, people were so intimately acquainted, they knew what everyone else needed. And when they had the ability to meet the requirement, whether it was a financial need met by selling possessions, a physical need met with a meal, or a spiritual need met at the altar in prayer, the need-meeter went to the need-needer. They gave and received with glad and generous hearts.

Did you catch that part? They RECEIVED with a generous heart. Does that seem strange to you? Generosity is normally associated with the giver, not the receiver. And receiving with a GLAD heart? We are more likely to receive with shame, reluctance, or a sense of obligation that we'll have to return the favor.

In true community, there is no shame in receiving. People give and receive generously because there is no expectation for a return. No. Scratch that. People give and receive generously because there IS an expectation for a return. There is an expectation that if you are able to meet a need, you will.

So find (or create!) a community where you can connect. Where you are giving when you have something to offer and receiving what others have to offer you. A place where you can show your glad and generous heart.

What will it take for you to find or create a community like this?

Are you able to receive generously from your community?

TOUGH GRACE
HELPS US
IMPROVE
WITHOUT
QUESTIONING
OUR
COMMITMENT OR
COMPETENCE

WHEN GRACE MUST BE TOUGH

What shall we say then? Are we to continue in sin that grace may abound? By no means! How can we who died to sin still live in it?
Romans 6:1-2 (ESV)

Recently, I had a mix-up on appointment times with a client. When I apologized for my mistake, she said the magic words.

"There is grace here."

Grace gets thrown around a lot these days. It's a spiritual practice that can be abused in our everyday lives.

Rather than always offering an easy, free-flowing grace that can lose its value, perhaps we need some accountability ... some tough grace.

In our roles as ministry and business leaders, where have we gone too far in letting grace abound?

Shall we continue to be late for appointments because we lose track of time?

Shall we continue to fall short of our commitments because things didn't go as planned?

Shall we continue to lose focus because we can't prioritize the most important tasks?

May it never be! We can offer ourselves grace, accept it from those around us and hold each other accountable, but we need a tough grace.

Tough grace says, "I understand where you are, but I love you too much to let you stay there." It gets down in the muck and helps you dig out, rather than letting you just bemoan your situation.

When a project doesn't give the results we expected, tough grace helps us look realistically at what happened. Did we really give it our full effort? Did we allow enough time to do it right? Did we approach it with the right spirit? Tough grace helps us improve without questioning our commitment or competence.

I'm thankful for the people in my life who offer me tough grace. They are in tune with what I'm trying to do, but also understand the other limitations in my life. They don't let me use limitations as excuses, but rather, as opportunities to fully rely on Jesus for the results.

Forward Thinking

Who are the people in your life that offer you tough grace and how does it help you complete the mission God has given you?

Resources for Finding Your People

Visit www.doanewthing.com/gogetter for additional resources related to this book.

Download the **Better Together Collaboration Guide**

Access the **"Creating Community"** video training

Get an **Accountability Check-in** worksheet

Do the Thing

You can dream the dreams, make some plans, and find the people, but the most vulnerable step you'll ever take is when you Do The Thing. The hard work you've put in will shine under the spotlight ... or the light will expose some harsh realities. You'll want to celebrate one minute and feel like quitting the next.

But that's normal. Any worthy work has its ups and downs. The life or death of your dream depends on how you handle these rolling waves. Will you fold at the first sign of resistance? Or will you keep moving forward?

If I know anything about you, you'll do the thing.

AS YOU PREPARE
TO TAKE YOUR
FIRST STEP,
THE RIGHT TIME
TO TAKE IT IS
WHEN THE
WATERS AROUND
YOUR IDEA ARE
STIRRING AND
INTEREST IS
HIGH

FEAR-BUSTING TIPS TO TAKE YOUR FIRST STEP

… whoever then first, after the stirring up of the water, stepped in was made well. John 5:4 (NIV)

Baby steps are the cutest, aren't they? A little wobbly, fear mixed with pride and sprinkled with excitement. As parents and grandparents, grownups who have taken millions of steps, we can't imagine what goes on in that little baby's head.

What if I let go of this table and fall down?
Why is this going so slow?
I bet I look silly doing this.

Ok, maybe not that last one.

Those first steps are tiny and huge all at the same time. They signify growth, confidence and a new phase of life. All of that from something that is second nature to the rest of us. But sometimes, it takes a little push on that diapered hiney to put one foot in front of the other.

If you are about to take the first steps toward a passion that God has put on your heart, you may be feeling the same way …. a little wobby, fear mixed with pride and sprinkled with excitement.

There was a man sitting by a pool in Bethesda who also needed help taking that first step.

Everyone at Bethesda was waiting for the right time to take their step. They watched expectantly for the Angel of the Lord to start stirring the waters. Maybe they shared tips with each other … the quickest way to get in the pool or the spot where the stirring was the strongest.

As you prepare to take your first step, the right time to take it is when the waters around your idea are stirring and interest is high.

When you take that step in obedience, Jesus will make things happen. You aren't depending on yourself, how fast you can get in the water or what is going to happen when you get there. You are solely dependent on God and can trust him for results.

And whether those results from your first step are tiny or huge, that little ripple of excitement in your soul will give you the confidence you need to take the next step.

Forward Thinking

What is your first (or next) step?

Is this the right time to take it?

WHAT IF WE
SIMPLY
STARTED ...⊠
AND STARTED
SIMPLE?

THE POWER OF STARTING SIMPLE

"For I know the plans I have for you, plans to prosper you and not to harm you, plans to give you hope and a future." Jeremiah 29:11 (NIV)

It started out as a simple idea, really. Or maybe not so much an idea, as a calling.

God said, "Create something."

Or, "Help someone."

Or, "Go somewhere."

And so we started. Or tried to start.

What we thought was simple became complicated. There was technology to learn and advice from so many placest to implement. Could's and should's and must do's to be successful crowded out the idea. As our to-do lists got longer, we moved farther and farther from the simple thing we weree trying to do.

What if we tried something different? What if we simply started …. and started simple? There's a freedom in starting when you don't know the "right" way to do things.

We are free to write from the heart without the structure of scannable headings and numbered lists.

We can create from our imaginations in any color or font we like.

We can build relationships with kindred spirits whether there is mutual benefit or not.

Starting simple is surprisingly difficult. We have to be disciplined to stay off the crazy train that compares our beginning to someone else's end and finds it lacking. We must be comfortable in our simplicity, knowing that time and patience may bring growth not measured in followers, page views, or sales.

Starting simple does not mean we don't have big dreams. Our time spent starting simple can also be a time of intentional learning that sets us up for success. We learn one step at a time until we look back and are amazed at what has become of that simple idea.

I have ideas for new ways to support and encourage God's girls who are making Him famous online. That is the simple thing God has called me to do, so I'll start these new things one simple step at a time.

If God has given you a big dream, don't wait until you have it all figured out. Start simple and grow into your dream. Or if your simple start became overly complicated and you got stuck, go back to the beginning, start simple again, and move forward from there. There is power in simply starting.

Forward Thinking

What simple dream have you made too complicated?

How can you scale it back and simply start?

JESUS MODELED
FOR US HOW TO
STEP OUT OF OUR
COMFORT ZONES
TO DELIVER THE
MESSAGE THE
WAY PEOPLE NEED
TO HEAR IT.

MAXIMIZING THE MESSAGE

And He got into one of the boats, which was Simon's, and asked him to put out a little way from the land. And He sat down and began teaching the people from the boat. Luke 5:3 (NASB)

Jesus is often described as a radical, and there was nothing more radical than the way He communicated with people. The other religious leaders of the day taught in one place … in the synagogue. They stood in the temple preaching from the text to the righteous people who faithfully attended.

But what about those who would never step foot in a temple? Or who were so consumed by the brokenness in their own lives that the condemnation of breaking one of the thousands of laws would send them right. over. the. edge?

Jesus did not shun them, or consider them unworthy of His limited time and energy. He went to them, spoke in their own common language, and focused on their needs first. He preached to large crowds. (Matthew 5) He lived life in social events. (Luke 7) He reached out one-on-one. (Luke 19) He even wrote and drew in the sand. (John 8) (Could this have been the very first social media Scripture graphic?) And yes, He preached in the temple. (John 7)

Jesus is perfect and fully God, but while He was on earth, He was also fully human and had a personality with likes and dislikes just like us. The Gospels are full of references to Jesus withdrawing from the crowds to rest and pray. I like to think He may have been an introvert like me. Maybe He was much more comfortable relating one-on-one with women at wells and men in trees than He was preaching to thousands on a hillside. But He put His personal preferences aside to reach the people His Father put in front of Him.

His message was always the same. You matter. Follow me. Love each other. But Jesus modeled for us how to step out of our comfort zones to deliver the message the way people need to hear it.

Forward Thinking

What are your favorite and least favorite ways to deliver your message?

How could your target audience be better served by delivering your message in a different way or format?

Will you get uncomfortable to reach them?

GOD HAS NOT
FORGOTTEN THE
PROMISE HE
MADE TO US OR
THE ONE WE
MADE TO HIM.

WAIT FOR WHAT LINGERS

Write down the revelation and make it plain on tablets so that a herald may run with it. For the revelation awaits an appointed time; it speaks of the end and will not prove false. Though it linger, wait for it; it will certainly come and will not delay.
Habakkuk 2:2-3 (NIV)

How do you react when you haven't made as much progress as you hoped?

We are so passionate about our dreams. When we start thinking about them, in our minds, we can drop everything else and focus on them. We can devote hours to working on them.

But then real life happens. We get distracted. Our other important responsibilities suddenly become urgent. Things don't move as quickly as we expect. And when that dream becomes the fourth or fifth thing we think of as we face each day, instead of the first, the passion ebbs, life crowds in, and we can hardly remember why that idea was so all-consuming important in the first place.

That's why God says write it down. He tells us to write it in stone, so it won't get lost or forgotten. Because on those days when the dream is dim and it is taking longer than we expected, we need a solid place ... a marker ... to remind us.

God has not forgotten the promise He made to us or the one we made to Him. We just need to be patient and wait. Wait for His appointed time. Wait for Him to come through. Wait through the lingering. But waiting is hard and we don't like it.These verses in Habakkuk remind us that what God has shown us may be the end. He sees what we don't see coming. The fact that we don't see it doesn't make it any less true.

When we get bogged down waiting in the messy, sometimes mundane, middle, it is easy to feel like the end will never get here. But God has an appointed time for the end. So wait for it. He will certainly come through. God said so.

What ending has God shown you that may look impossible now?

Write it down and put it somewhere as a reminder of what God has promised.

WE CAN FIND
GOD'S BLESSING
IN THE CHANGE
AND EMBRACE
WHAT HE IS
DOING.

WHEN UNEXPECTED CHANGE ROCKS YOUR WORLD

My soul magnifies the Lord, and my spirit rejoices in God my Savior, for he has looked on the humble estate of his servant. For behold, from now on all generations will call me blessed. Luke 1:46-48 (ESV)

There once was a girl named Mary. She was excited as she faced changes in her life. Engaged to the dreamy Joseph, she couldn't wait to spend the rest of her life as his beloved wife.

But God had a different change in mind for our girl, Mary. God chose Mary bring His Son into the world.

When Mary heard the news, she was perplexed. I can imagine her brows furrowed and her mouth hung open as she asked the messenger how this could be! Painful conversations with Joseph and her family flashed before her eyes. Shame immediately crept in as she wondered what her community would think. Surely, they would not understand.

And fear. Oh, the fear of suddenly becoming a mother, of the great responsibility and of the unknown future for herself and her son. There was no guidebook for being the mother of the Son of God.

The messenger reassured her that this unfathomable change was actually a gift from the Holy Spirit. That she was part of the holy unfolding of God's plan that would go on for eternity. Mary began to see the blessing in this change. She looked past the immediate pain to glimpse what God was doing and she chose to be a willing participant. She held fast to her deep belief that God is good and she rejoiced in Him.

Friends, you probably know by now that one of the only certainties in life is that things will change. Change, even good, happy change, always brings an element of pain. We may not be able to control the change life thrusts upon us, but we can control how we react to it. Instead of letting that pain derail our plans and sour our outlooks, we can find God's blessing in the change and embrace what He is doing.

What changes are threatening to derail your plans?

How will you choose to navigate change?

OUR TRUST IS
NOT IN OUR
PLANS. WE
TRUST IN THE
GREATNESS AND
AWESOMENESS
OF OUR LORD

MANAGE THE RISKS

And I looked and arose and said to the nobles and to the officials and to the rest of the people, Do not be afraid of them. Remember the Lord, who is great and awesome, and fight for your brothers, your sons, your daughters, your wives, and your homes. Nehemiah 4:14 (ESV)

Nehemiah was busy, leading the Israelites as they rebuilt the crumbling wall around Jerusalem. It was a risky endeavor. The enemies around them were used to being able to attack the city at will. In fact, Nehemiah got word that his enemies were planning to sabotage his efforts.

The rumors and fear were distracting the workers. Morale was low and commitment to the task was waning. Nehemiah didn't wait until the enemies attacked. He recognized this as a risk to the work God had called him to do, and he put in place a plan to manage the risk.

Nehemiah stationed half the workers near the low places in the wall and armed them with swords, spears, and bows. It slowed down the work, but when the workers felt safe, they were more productive and made more progress on the wall.

But then ... Nehemiah went before the people and reminded them of the greatness and awesomeness of the Lord. They may have weapons in hand, but it would be the Lord who would stand with them and protect their families.

This reminds me of the verses in Ephesians where Paul instructs us to put on the full armor of God and then "having done all, stand firm." We can put armor around our ministries by planning for potential risks, but in the end, having done all, we can stand firm.

It is wise to plan for how we would handle things that may go wrong. But our trust is not in our plans. We trust in the greatness and awesomeness of our Lord to protect us from the people and circumstances that may derail us.

Forward Thinking

What are the greatest risks your ministry or business face right now?

What steps can you take to reduce the risk?

What promise has God given to help you stand firm?

SO DO THE
WORK FINISH
THE WORK AND
DON'T BE
DISCOURAGED

MINISTRY IS HARD, SO DO THE WORK

Be strong and courageous, and do the work. Do not be afraid or discouraged, for the Lord God, my God, is with you. He will not fail you or forsake you until all the work for the service of the temple of the Lord is finished. 1 Chronicles 28:20 (NIV)

Ministry is hard. Is that a revelation to anyone besides me?

Just before David's death, he handed the reins to his son, Solomon, and the verses above were the last advice this great king gave to a future great king.

I don't know about you, but that makes me shake in my flip flops a little bit! You might think a father would give his son some fluffy final words … "You are awesome, you'll be a great king, you are ready for this, it will be easy!"

But no. David knew better. After battling Goliath, Saul, and the consequences of his own sin, David knew being a king was hard and it would take every bit of strength and courage his son could muster up. He also knew it would take one more thing. Work.

Ministry is messy. Serving people takes guts and a thick skin. It can be lonely when most of what we do is never seen. Ministry most definitely takes work.

So do the work. Hone your craft and expand your knowledge and experience. Get over your own insecurities and false humility to share the amazing gifts God has planted in you.

Maybe you are saying (or whining), "But I AM doing the work! I'm up late writing after the kids go to bed. I take courses, get advice, sacrifice time and money I could spend on my family, and NOTHING is happening!" Then I have good news for you.

Ministry is hard, but *"Do not be afraid or discouraged, for the Lord God, my God, is with you."*

When we give in to the fear and discouragement, we forget the Lord our God is with us, just as He was with David and Solomon. We forget He started this thing and He will finish it.

Ministry is hard, so finish the work. *"He will not fail or forsake you until ALL the work for the service of the temple of the Lord is finished."*

Is that a promise you need to grab hold of today? God, who gifts you, inspires you, and gives you all the resources you need to complete your assignment, will not fail or forsake you until ALL of the work is FINISHED! He is not giving up on us, even if we are tempted to give up on the work.

And guess what …. I have a sneaking suspicion that as soon as this work is finished, He's got another assignment waiting with my name on it. And one with your name on it, too.

So DO the work. FINISH the work. And don't be discouraged. The Lord God, **MY** God, **YOUR** God, will be with you.

Forward Thinking

Which part of ministry is hardest for you?

How can God meet you in that difficult place?

Resources for Doing Your Thing

Visit www.doanewthing.com/gogetter for additional resources related to this book.

Download the **Christian Blogger's Content Idea Library**

Join the **Move Forward Mastermind**

Contact me for **one-on-one coaching**

Thank you for hanging with me through the end of this book. My prayer is that your vision has been expanded, your confidence has increased, and your spirit has been renewed.

More than anything else, I hope your restless, go-getter soul has found a resting place in God's Word. We can be peacefully busy instead of falling into the hustle culture. We can have God's best without having it all … whatever "all" is. We can make imperfect progress in the midst of God's perfect plan.

There's nothing wrong with being a go-getter. God wired us to pursue purpose and passion. But in the going and getting, we must remember that we are first Jesus girls. It will be His grace and good favor that keep us moving forward.

Let's continue the conversation!

- Visit me at DoANewThing.com and become part of the community.
- Follow me (@doanewthing) on Facebook and Instagram.
- Leave an honest review of *Moving Forward* on Amazon to help others find it.

P.S. Many of these devotions were taken from my signature program, the Move Forward Mastermind. The mastermind is a 12-week program that combines Biblical principles with skills from the project management world to help you complete your most important goals and projects. If you'd like to learn more about the practical tools and training that go with the spiritual lessons from this book, please visit https://doanewthing.com/moveforward

Praise for Do A New Thing

Thanks to Christa and Do A New Thing, I am getting things done! I love her organizational tools and products, as well as her one-on-one coaching. Do A New Thing has been a key tool for my ministry.

Kristine Brown
Founder of More Than Yourself, Inc. and author of
Over It: Conquering Comparison to Live Out God's Plan

If you need help with growing your ministry, or just gaining control of your schedule, Christa is who you want!! No where else can you get the support and encouragement that will help propel you forward. And Christa accomplishes it all with grace, integrity, and professionalism, as well as a heart for each person she works with.

Erin Peters
Director of Women and Worship at Fort St. John Alliance Church

Christa's attention to detail, strategic thinking, and dedication to excellence are strengths that have been invaluable to me in ministry. She is a team player who has what it takes to move a ministry from good to great.

Melissa Taylor
Director of First 5 and Online Bible Studies, Proverbs 31 Ministries

God led me to Christa at just the right time. She shares knowledge and guides you in such a clear way. Every meeting I've had with her has blown my mind in terms of all we accomplished and the giant step forward she took with me.

Judy Mills
Founder, Radiant.NYC

Hello, Dream.
Meet
Reality

Strategy Development

Accountability Coaching

Project Management

for Christian Communicators & Leaders

Girl, you've been circling this mountain long enough.

Move Forward

Are you ready to ...

Accomplish the goals you've had too long?

Get focused and organized?

Connect with a tough grace community?

Trade your to-do list for a got-it-done list?

MOVE FORWARD

MASTERMIND

Join the Move Forward Mastermind and learn

the skills you need to manage the tasks that

matter and reach your most important goals.

www.doanewthing.com/moveforward

use the code MOVE20 to take $20 off the
membership fee

54074273R00074

Made in the
USA
Lexington, KY